Water Works!

Written by:
Sharon Brinkerhoff

Illustrated by: **Liliane Grenier**

An Original Playbook®

presented in….

Playbook® Advantage Format

© 2010 Playbooks, Inc., ALL RIGHTS RESERVED.

RS 0-2
GLC PK-1
Story Length: 498 Words

Water Works

PUBLISHED BY PLAYBOOKS, INC.
d.b.a. Playbooks Reader's Theater

Copyright © 2010 by Playbooks, Inc., Lake Forest, CA.
All Rights Reserved.

Playbook, Playbooks, Playbook Format, Roleplay Reader,
Playberized, StageBooks, and Being a Start Makes Reading Fun
are trademarks of Playbook, Inc.

ISBN 978-1-60476-083-5

The unique format of a Playbook® with character colorization and specialized readability levels is a proprietary method of book structure, writing, format, construction, re-construction, displaying and printing protected under U.S. Patent Nos. 6,683,611, 6,859,206, and 7,456,834 with additional patents pending. For information regarding licensing the rights to write, edit, construct, re-construct, display, print or publish any book in Playbook® format call 1-800-375-2926. No part of this publication may be reproduced in whole or in part, or stored in a retrieval system, or transmitted in any form or by any means, electronic, mechanical, photocopying, recording, or otherwise, without written permission of the publisher, except by a reviewer, who may quote brief passages in a review. For information regarding permission, call Playbooks, Inc. at 1-800-375-2926. This book is subject to the condition that it shall not, by way of trade or otherwise, be re-sold, hired out, or otherwise circulated without the publisher's prior consent in any form of binding or cover other than that in which it is published and without a similar condition including this condition being imposed on the subsequent purchaser. Performances of this story/script may be videotaped for school or library purposes.

Being a Star Makes Reading Fun™

Welcome to the world of Playbooks® and the beginning of a wonderful role-play reading adventure! Playbook® stories are presented in a unique and colorful format and are read out loud by several readers like a play, without memorization, props, or a stage. When you read a Playbook®, you and other readers bring the story to life and become the characters. As you read **your** part out loud, you will have fun expressing and acting like your character. You and the other readers will explore the story plot together and learn what will happen next. It's an exciting journey of discovery that pulls you into the story, and you'll want to read it out loud again and again!

HOW TO GET STARTED

Begin your reading adventure with the **Character Summary** here at the beginning of the book. **You'll notice right away that the words and sentences for each character appear in a different color here and throughout the book. This will make it easy to follow along and read your part with confidence and enthusiasm.**

It doesn't matter whether you are a beginning reader or an experienced reader; there is a part for everyone. The number of characters in the story may not match the number of readers in your group and that's okay. Readers can play more than one character role, or readers can share a role by taking turns.

Once your role has been assigned, you and the other readers will each read his or her character's summary out loud from his or her own copy of the book. The most experienced reader typically reads the narrator's role.
It's important for teachers and parents to refer to the Teacher or Parent Guide when assigning roles.

Have fun bringing your character to life by bringing your voice up and down, speaking softly or loudly, changing your facial expressions, and moving your hands or body. Trying different voices or accents can also be lots of fun.

Sometimes you will see *black italicized text* inside parenthesis before or in the middle of sentences. **These are called "cues" and tell you how to read a sentence with expression.** For example, if the "cue" says *(with surprise),* speak the sentence with surprise in your voice! Cues are not read out loud.

MAKING THE MOST OF THE STORY

It's more fun to read the story out loud together with other readers the first time you read your role. It's exciting to discover the story in this way rather than each reader practicing his or her part alone first. As you get better with your role, you may want to change the way you express your character's personality, or you may want to switch roles with another reader. Be creative! When all your readers get comfortable with their roles, you may want to read the story in front of a friendly audience.

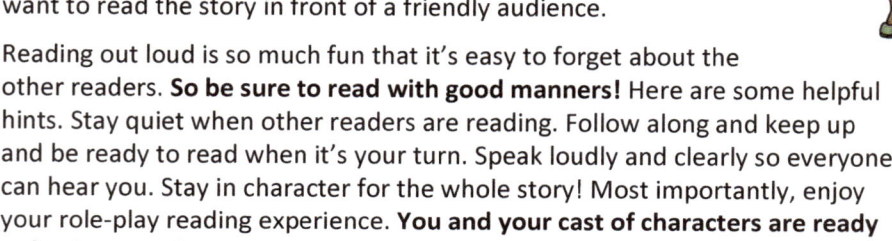

Reading out loud is so much fun that it's easy to forget about the other readers. **So be sure to read with good manners!** Here are some helpful hints. Stay quiet when other readers are reading. Follow along and keep up and be ready to read when it's your turn. Speak loudly and clearly so everyone can hear you. Stay in character for the whole story! Most importantly, enjoy your role-play reading experience. **You and your cast of characters are ready to begin your Playbook® adventure!**

FOR TEACHERS AND PARENTS

For specific guidance on implementing a Playbook® story in the classroom or in the home, download a FREE Teacher or Parent Guide at the following link.
http://www.readerstheater.com/teacherguide.pdf

It's important for students to be assigned a role they can read with success in front of their peers. A "Recommended Reader Assignment" chart that identifies the reading level for each story character is included in this story's group set. To print additional copies, visit www.readerstheater.com/rra.html **and locate the story's title.**

Being an active participant in a story spikes the reader's curiosity to learn more about the story's theme. Rewarding a child for exceptional effort and performance is an excellent practice for boosting a child's reading confidence. To download **FREE Award Certificates** to recognize star performers, visit www.readerstheater.com/awardcertificates.pdf.

Playbooks, Inc. also provides story-specific activity suggestions and worksheets to reinforce concepts and go beyond the story into the content areas of Language Arts, Math, Science, Social Studies, Art, Health, etc., as well as Character Development. Activities range in skill level and age-appropriateness, so the teacher or parent can choose activities that best suit the readers. Activities include comprehension quizzes, crossword puzzles, word search, vocabulary, discussion and writing prompts, story mapping, word problems, etc. To download FREE supplemental activity sheets for this and other stories, visit www.readerstheater.com/supplements.html.

Seeing children develop a passion for reading while working with the Playbook® format will be one of your greatest rewards.

Character Summary

Before beginning this story, it is helpful for each reader to read his/her character's summary *aloud*.

Max
I like to play at the park. I like to drink soda pop.

Jack
I like to play ball. I like my dog.

Ann
I like to play, too. I like my cat.

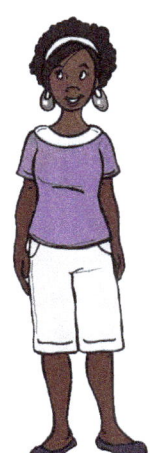

Mrs. Jon
I like to make sure my children are healthy and happy!

Max	My tummy is sick. So what can I do?
Jack	You do not look good.
Ann	Yes, I think so, too.
Mrs. Jon	You drank so much soda pop! So, that could be why.
Ann	I saw him do it.

Jack	Yes, so did I.
Mrs. Jon	Come try some water. Soda Pop's bad for you.
Max	Then I will try it.
Ann	It is good to do.
Jack	I like it. I'll have some.
Ann	And I'll have some, too.

Mrs. Jon	I'll get it for you.
Max	Well, okay, thank you!
Mrs. Jon	Soda pop dries you out, so you think you need more.
Max	Did I drink many cans?
Jack	Yes! We saw you have four!
Mrs. Jon	We need water to live. Plants need it to grow.

Ann	I like it.
Jack	Me, too.
Max	I can see it is so.
Mrs. Jon	Do you all take baths?
Ann	Yes, I do!
Jack	And me, too.
Mrs. Jon	It's the water that cleans you.
Max	I know it is true.
Mrs. Jon	Do you take baths in soda pop?
Ann	I do not!
Jack	No, not me!
Mrs. Jon	You would not get clean.

Max	That is easy to see.
Mrs. Jon	Did you know that to drink is like taking a bath?
Max	On the inside, right?
Mrs. Jon	Now you're on the right path.
Max	Inside and outside.
Ann	Outside and in.

Mrs. Jon	They both need to be clean, and then we all win. We need water for cleaning inside us each day.
Jack	It feels good.
Ann	For me, too.
Max	It is the best way.
Ann	I think I want more.
Jack	More for me.
Max	Please, me, too.

Mrs. Jon	Yes, keep drinking water.
Jack	It is so good to do.
Mrs. Jon	There is still more to tell.
Ann	What is it?
Jack	Please tell me.
Mrs. Jon	Our bodies need water to be really healthy.

Mrs. Jon	More than half of our body is water, it's true.
Ann	I can not see it.
Max	It is hard to do.
Mrs. Jon	It's inside us and hidden, but sometimes comes out.
Max	That is something for sure I want to know about.
Mrs. Jon	Have you ever been running and saw that you sweat?
Max	All the time!
Jack	Yes, I do.
Ann	And I can get wet!

Mrs. Jon	That is the water inside coming out!
Max	It must go back in!
Mrs. Jon	That's what drinking's about. There's one way to tell if you're drinking enough.
Jack	What is it?

Ann	Please tell us.
Max	I like learning this stuff!
Mrs. Jon	You can tell by your mouth. A wet mouth is a good sign.
Jack	Mine is wet.
Ann	Mine is, too.
Max	Mine is wet. I feel fine!
Ann	Mine used to be dry and my tummy felt bad.
Jack	And now you feel good.

Mrs. Jon	We are so very glad. The pop dried you out. It was water you lacked.
Max	But now I am better, and will be right back.
Ann	Where did he go?
Jack	We will just have to see.

Mrs. Jon   Even to me, it's a mystery.

Max   Now that is much better! I feel so good.
Ann   What did you do?
Max   I pooped, now that I could!

Jack	Ha ha, you said poop!
Ann	And now you did, too!
Mrs. Jon	But it's just a word. Something we all do.
Max	From now on I drink water. I will not drink pop.
Jack	You will like it.
Mrs. Jon	So, don't ever stop!

The End

www.ingramcontent.com/pod-product-compliance
Lightning Source LLC
Chambersburg PA
CBHW061806070526
44586CB00023B/2740